Rise Up and Shine: Unlocking Your Potential for Success

Are you feeling stuck in your life, lacking motivation or direction? Do you dream of achieving big goals, but don't know where to start? If so, this Book is for you.

Rise Up and Shine is a motivational guide that will help you unlock your full potential and take your life to the next level. Through inspiring stories, practical exercises and insightful tips, you'll learn how to overcome obstacles, cultivate a positive mindset, and develop the habits of successful people.

You'll discover:

- The power of self-belief and positive thinking
- Strategies for setting and achieving goals
- How to overcome fear, doubt, and negative self-talk
- Techniques for boosting your confidence and resilience
- Ways to build healthy relationships and networks
- Tips for creating work-life balance and managing stress
- You will also find practical exercises, quizzes, and affirmations to help you stay motivated and on track, and to measure your progress along the way.
- And much more!

Whether you're an aspiring entrepreneur, a career professional, a student, or simply someone who wants to live a more fulfilling life, this book will provide you with the inspiration and guidance you need to succeed.

So, if you're ready to rise up, shine, and make your dreams a reality, get your copy of Rise Up and Shine today!

Index

- Prioritizing self-care
- Achieving work-life balance
- Stress-Management Quiz
- Stress-Management exercise

Chapter 7: Reflection and Growth
- Taking time for reflection
- Making necessary adjustments to your plan of action
- Measuring progress and celebrating successes
- Measuring progress quiz
- self-evaluation Quiz
- Self-reflection exercise

Chapter 1: Understanding Your Potential

Recognizing your strengths and weaknesses

Recognizing our strengths and weaknesses is an important step in personal and professional development. Here are some ways to identify them:

1. **Self-reflection:** Take time to reflect on your experiences, accomplishments, and areas for improvement. Think about what comes naturally to you and where you struggle.

2. **Feedback:** Ask trusted friends, family members, or colleagues for honest feedback about your strengths and weaknesses. Be open to constructive criticism and use it to improve.

3. **Assessments:** Take personality or skills assessments to gain insight into your strengths and weaknesses. Examples include the Myers-Briggs Type Indicator, Clifton Strengths, and DISC Assessment.

4. **Observation**: Observe yourself in various situations to identify patterns in your behavior. For example, do you thrive in social situations or prefer to work independently?

By understanding your strengths and weaknesses, you can set realistic goals, improve your performance, and make better decisions.

Identifying your values and priorities

Identifying your values and priorities can help you focus on what truly matters to you, and guide you in making decisions that align with your goals and aspirations. Here are some steps to help you

identify your values and priorities:

1. **Reflect on what is important to you**: Think about the things that bring you the most joy and fulfillment, and what you would like to achieve in life. Ask yourself questions such as: What do I enjoy doing? What am I passionate about? What motivates me?

2. **Make a list of your values:** Write down the values that are most important to you. For example, your values might include things like honesty, integrity, kindness, compassion, creativity, or adventure.

3. **Prioritize your values**: Once you have a list of your values, prioritize them in order of importance. This will help you identify which values are most essential to your overall sense of well-being.

4. **Evaluate your current priorities:** Think about how you are currently spending your time and energy. Are your actions and decisions aligned with your values and priorities? If not, consider making changes to bring your life into greater alignment with what truly matters to you.

5. **Revisit your values and priorities regularly:** Our values and priorities can change over time, so it's important to revisit them regularly to ensure that they are still relevant and meaningful to us. Set aside time each year to reflect on your values and priorities and make any necessary adjustments.

Chapter 2: Setting and Achieving Goals

Defining your goals

Defining your goals is an important step in achieving success. To define your goals, you should first consider your long-term aspirations and then break them down into smaller, more achievable objectives. This process will help you create a clear roadmap for achieving your goals and provide you with a sense of direction. When defining your goals, it's important to make them specific, measurable, achievable, relevant, and time-bound (SMART). This means that your goals should be well-defined, quantifiable, realistic, relevant to your life and values, and have a clear timeline for completion.

Additionally, it's important to consider the potential obstacles and challenges that you may face along the way and develop a plan for how to overcome them. This will help you stay focused and motivated, even when faced with setbacks or roadblocks.

Remember, goal setting is not a one-time event, but rather an ongoing process. As you progress and achieve your objectives, it's important to revisit and revise your goals to ensure that they remain relevant and aligned with your values and aspirations.

Breaking down your goals into actionable steps

Breaking down your goals into actionable steps involves breaking down your overall goals into smaller, more manageable tasks or milestones. This can help you stay focused and motivated, as you can see progress being made towards your larger goals.

To break down your goals into actionable steps, you can follow these steps:

1. Start with your end goal in mind. What is the ultimate outcome you are trying to achieve? Write it down.

2. Identify the major milestones or steps required to reach your end goal. These are the major accomplishments you need to achieve in order to move closer to your end goal.

3. Break down each milestone into smaller, more manageable tasks. These tasks should be specific, measurable, and time-bound.

4. Create a timeline for each task. Assign a deadline for each task and create a timeline that outlines when each task should be completed.

5. Review and adjust your plan as needed. Regularly review your progress and adjust your plan as needed to ensure you stay on track.

Remember to keep your goals SMART (specific, measurable, achievable, relevant, and time-bound) and to celebrate each milestone you achieve along the way.

Tracking your progress

Tracking your progress is an essential aspect of goal achievement. It helps you to stay motivated, make necessary adjustments, and celebrate your successes. Here are some tips for tracking your progress:

1. **Keep a journal:** Write down your goals and track your progress regularly. You can use a physical journal or an online tool.

2. **Set milestones:** Break down your goals into smaller milestones and track your progress towards each milestone. Celebrate each milestone achieved.

3. **Use metrics:** Use metrics to measure your progress. For example, if your goal is to lose weight, track your weight loss progress and body measurements.

4. **Use visual aids:** Create a visual representation of your progress. For example, use a graph or chart to show your progress over time.

5. **Adjust your plan:** If you are not making progress, adjust your plan. Identify the barriers and find ways to overcome them.

Remember, tracking your progress is an ongoing process. Make it a habit to track your progress regularly, and you will be on your way to achieving your goals.

Gratitude Journal:

Instructions: Create a new document or notebook dedicated to your gratitude journal. Each day, write down at least three things you are grateful for. These can be big or small things, moments, people, experiences, or even simple pleasures. Try to be as specific and detailed as possible.

Example: Date: March 10th, 2023
Today I am grateful for:
1. The warm cup of coffee I had this morning that gave me a boost of energy to start my day.
2. The supportive and encouraging words from my colleague that helped me to feel more confident about my work.
3. The beautiful sunset I saw on my way home that reminded me of the beauty and wonder of the world.

Remember to take a few moments each day to reflect on the positive things in your life and express gratitude for them. Over time, this practice can help to cultivate a more positive and optimistic outlook on life.

Goal-setting quiz:

Here's a sample goal-setting quiz:
1. What is a SMART goal?
   a) A goal that is specific, measurable, achievable, relevant, and timely
   b) A goal that is simple, meaningful, accurate, realistic, and transparent
   c) A goal that is strategic, manageable, adaptable, reliable, and truthful

2. Why is it important to set goals?
   a) To provide direction and purpose
   b) To increase motivation and focus
   c) All of the above

3. What is the difference between short-term and long-term goals?
   a) Short-term goals can be achieved in a matter of days or weeks, while long-term goals take months or years to accomplish.
   b) Short-term goals are less important than long-term goals.
   c) Long-term goals are often related to personal development, while short-term goals are related to everyday tasks.

4. What is an example of a short-term goal?
   a) Running a marathon
   b) Saving for retirement
   c) Completing a project by the end of the week

5. What is an example of a long-term goal?
   a) Getting a promotion within the next six months
   b) Traveling the world within the next year
   c) Starting a business within the next five years

Answers:
1.   a) A goal that is specific, measurable, achievable, relevant, and timely
2.   c) All of the above
3.   a) Short-term goals can be achieved in a matter of days or

weeks, while long-term goals take months or years to accomplish.

4. c) Completing a project by the end of the week
5. c) Starting a business within the next five years

Gratitude exercise

here's a simple gratitude exercise you can try:

1. Find a quiet and comfortable place to sit or lie down.
2. Close your eyes and take a few deep breaths to relax your mind and body.
3. Start by bringing to mind something you are grateful for in your life. It can be anything, big or small, that brings you joy or happiness.
4. Once you have identified something, focus on it for a few moments. Try to really feel the emotions associated with it, and think about how it has positively impacted your life.
5. From there, begin to expand your focus to other things you are grateful for. These can be people, experiences, material possessions, or anything else that you appreciate in your life.
6. Spend a few minutes focusing on each of these things, allowing yourself to really feel the gratitude and positivity associated with them.
7. When you feel ready, slowly open your eyes and take a few deep breaths before returning to your day.

You can repeat this exercise daily or as often as you like, and it can be a powerful tool for shifting your mindset towards positivity

Goal-setting exercise:

Here's a goal-setting exercise you can try:

1. **Identify your long-term goal:** Start by identifying what you want to achieve in the long-term. This could be a career goal, a personal goal, a health and fitness goal, or any other goal that you feel is important to you.

2. **Break down your goal into smaller, measurable steps:** Once you have identified your long-term goal, break it down into smaller, more manageable steps that you can measure and track. For example, if your goal is to run a marathon, your smaller steps could include running a certain number of miles each week, increasing your distance gradually, and tracking your progress using a running app.

3. **Set specific, achievable targets for each step:** For each step, set specific, achievable targets that you can realistically accomplish within a certain time frame. For example, if your step is to run a certain number of miles each week, set a target of running 5 miles per week for the first week, then gradually increasing it by 1-2 miles each week until you reach your target distance.

4. **Create a timeline:** Create a timeline for each step, setting deadlines for each target along the way. This will help you stay on track and hold yourself accountable.

5. **Track your progress:** Regularly track your progress and celebrate each milestone that you achieve. This will help you stay motivated and focused on your goal.

Remember to be flexible and adjust your plan as necessary. Goal-setting is a dynamic process and you may encounter obstacles or challenges along the way. Stay committed to your goal, keep a positive attitude, and never give up on your dreams.

Chapter 3: Overcoming Fear, Doubt, and Negative Self-Talk

In this chapter, we will explore different techniques to overcome fear, doubt, and negative self-talk, which can hinder your personal and professional growth. We will discuss:

- Strategies for conquering self-doubt
- Overcoming fear of failure
- Replacing negative self-talk with positive affirmations

By the end of this chapter, you will have a better understanding of how to identify and manage fear, doubt, and negative self-talk to achieve your goals and unlock your potential.

Strategies for conquering self-doubt

Self-doubt can be a significant roadblock to success, but there are several strategies you can use to conquer it. Here are some examples:

1. **Challenge your negative self-talk:** When you catch yourself thinking negatively, challenge those thoughts. Ask yourself if they are true or if you are just assuming the worst. Try to reframe those negative thoughts into positive ones.

2. **Practice self-compassion:** Be kind to yourself and treat yourself with the same compassion and understanding you would offer to a friend. Remember that making mistakes is a normal part of the learning process.

3. **Focus on your strengths:** When you focus on your strengths, you can gain confidence in your abilities and feel more capable of tackling challenges.

4. **Take action:** Taking action towards your goals, even if it's just small steps, can help you feel more in control and less

overwhelmed.

5. **Surround yourself with positive people:** Seek out the support and encouragement of people who uplift and inspire you, rather than those who bring you down.

By incorporating these strategies into your daily life, you can overcome self-doubt and unlock your potential for success.

Overcoming fear of failure

Overcoming fear of failure is a common struggle that many people face. Here are some strategies to help:

1. **Reframe failure as a learning opportunity:** Instead of seeing failure as a negative outcome, try to reframe it as a learning opportunity. Failure can be a chance to gain new insights, skills, and knowledge that can help you succeed in the future.

2. **Practice self-compassion:** Be kind to yourself and don't be too hard on yourself when you make mistakes or experience setbacks. Acknowledge that everyone fails at some point and it's a normal part of the growth process.

3. **Set realistic goals:** Setting unrealistic goals can set you up for failure and make it harder to bounce back from setbacks. Make sure your goals are challenging yet achievable, and break them down into smaller, manageable steps.

4. **Visualize success:** Visualize yourself succeeding and achieving your goals. This can help boost your confidence and motivation and make it easier to overcome fear and self-doubt.

5. **Take action:** Taking action is often the best way to overcome fear and self-doubt. Start by taking small steps towards your goals and gradually work your way up to bigger

challenges. Remember that progress, not perfection, is key.

Replacing negative self-talk with positive affirmations

we will explore the power of positive affirmations and how they can help to reframe negative self-talk into positive self-talk. Negative self-talk can be a major obstacle to success, as it can hold us back from taking risks and trying new things. By replacing negative self-talk with positive affirmations, we can build our confidence and self-belief, and overcome our fears and doubts.

Some strategies for using positive affirmations include:
- Identifying negative thoughts and beliefs that are holding us back
- Creating positive affirmations that counteract these negative thoughts and beliefs
- Repeating these positive affirmations daily, either through meditation or writing them down
- Using visualization techniques to imagine ourselves achieving our goals and affirming our capabilities

Examples of positive affirmations include:
- I am capable of achieving my goals
- I am worthy of success and happiness
- I trust in my abilities and instincts
- I am confident and resilient
- I embrace challenges as opportunities for growth

By practicing positive affirmations consistently, we can reprogram our minds to think more positively and overcome our fears and doubts.

positive affirmations exercise

Here are some positive affirmations that can help boost confidence and self-belief:
1. I am worthy and deserving of success.
2. I trust in my abilities to achieve my goals.
3. I am confident in who I am and what I can do.

4. I am capable of overcoming any obstacles that come my way.
5. I am grateful for my talents and strengths.
6. I am constantly learning and growing.
7. I believe in myself and my potential.
8. I have the courage to take risks and pursue my dreams.
9. I am in control of my thoughts and emotions.
10. I am worthy of love and respect, both from myself and others.

Repeating these affirmations daily can help to reprogram negative thought patterns and replace them with positive beliefs, ultimately boosting confidence and self-belief.

Chapter 4: Boosting Your Confidence and Resilience

In this chapter, we will explore various techniques and strategies for boosting your confidence and resilience. These skills are essential for overcoming obstacles, staying motivated, and achieving your goals.

Topics that will be covered in this chapter include:
- Techniques for building confidence
- Developing a growth mindset
- Building resilience in the face of adversity

end of this chapter, you will have a better understanding of how to cultivate confidence and resilience, and be better equipped to navigate the ups and downs of life.

Techniques for building confidence

Some techniques for building confidence that could be included in this chapter are:

1. **Visualizing success:** Visualization is a powerful tool that can help boost confidence. Encourage readers to picture themselves achieving their goals and feeling successful.

2. **Practicing self-care:** Taking care of oneself can help boost confidence. Encourage readers to prioritize self-care activities such as exercise, healthy eating, and getting enough sleep.

3. **Celebrating successes:** Celebrating even small successes can help boost confidence. Encourage readers to acknowledge and celebrate their achievements, no matter how small.

4. **Challenging negative thoughts:** Negative thoughts can undermine confidence. Encourage readers to challenge negative thoughts by questioning their validity and replacing them with

positive affirmations.

5. **Stepping outside of comfort zones:** Trying new things and taking risks can help build confidence. Encourage readers to take small steps outside of their comfort zones to build confidence gradually.

Developing a growth mindset

Developing a growth mindset involves cultivating the belief that you can improve your abilities and intelligence through hard work and dedication. Some techniques for building a growth mindset include:

1. **Embracing challenges:** Rather than avoiding difficult tasks, embrace them as opportunities to learn and grow.
2. **Practicing persistence:** Keep pushing forward, even when faced with obstacles or setbacks.
3. **Cultivating a love of learning:** Seek out new experiences and knowledge, and approach them with an open mind.
4. **Fostering a positive attitude:** Focus on the positive aspects of a situation and look for opportunities to learn and grow.
5. **Embracing failure:** Recognize that failure is a natural part of the learning process and use it as a chance to reflect, learn, and grow.
6. **Celebrating successes:** Take time to acknowledge your accomplishments and celebrate your progress.

Building resilience in the face of adversity

we will explore ways to build resilience, which is the ability to bounce back and adapt in the face of adversity. Some techniques that will be covered include:

6. **Developing a positive outlook:** One way to build resilience is to cultivate a positive outlook. This means focusing on the positive aspects of a situation, even in the face of difficulty. It

also involves reframing negative thoughts into more positive ones.

7. **Practicing self-care:** Taking care of yourself physically and mentally can help you build resilience. This includes getting enough sleep, eating a healthy diet, and engaging in regular exercise. It also means making time for self-care activities such as meditation, yoga, or reading.

8. **Building a support network:** Having a strong support network can help you build resilience. This may include family members, friends, or a therapist. It's important to have people you can turn to when you need help or support.

9. **Learning from past experiences:** Reflecting on past experiences and learning from them can help you build resilience. By looking at what worked and what didn't in the past, you can develop strategies for dealing with future challenges.

10. **Embracing change:** Change is a natural part of life, and building resilience means being able to adapt to change. This may mean learning new skills, taking on new challenges, or simply being open to new experiences.

By practicing these techniques, you can build your resilience and develop the ability to bounce back from adversity.

Resilience quiz

Here's a resilience quiz:

1. When faced with a setback or failure, I tend to:
   a) Give up and lose hope
   b) Become overwhelmed and stressed

c) Reframe the situation and look for opportunities to learn and grow

2. How do you approach challenges?
   a) Avoid them at all costs
   b) Tackle them with a negative mindset
   c) Embrace them as opportunities for growth and learning

3. How do you typically respond to change?
   a) Resistant and reluctant
   b) Anxious and stressed
   c) Curious and adaptable

4. How do you cope with stress?
   a) Ignoring it and hoping it will go away
   b) Engaging in unhealthy coping mechanisms like substance abuse or binge-eating
   c) Engaging in healthy coping mechanisms like exercise, meditation, or talking to a friend

5. How do you view failure?
   a) As a personal flaw or weakness
   b) As a sign of incompetence or lack of ability
   c) As an opportunity for growth and learning

Scoring: For each question, give yourself 1 point for "a", 2 points for "b", and 3 points for "c". Add up your points to determine your resilience score.

- 5-7 points: You may struggle with resilience and may benefit from developing some resilience-building strategies.
- 8-12 points: You have moderate resilience and may benefit from focusing on strengthening your resilience in specific areas.
- 13-15 points: You have a high level of resilience and likely have effective coping strategies in place to help you bounce back from challenges and setbacks.

Self-belief Quiz:

1. Do you believe that you have the ability to achieve your goals?
- Answer options: Yes, No, Sometimes, Not Sure

2. How often do you doubt your own abilities or self-worth?
- Answer options: Rarely, Sometimes, Often, Always

3. How do you respond to setbacks or failures?
- Answer options: Give up easily, Get discouraged but keep trying, Analyze what went wrong and try again, Use setbacks as opportunities to learn and grow

4. Do you often compare yourself to others, feeling inferior or inadequate?
- Answer options: Rarely, Sometimes, Often, Always

5. How confident do you feel when faced with new challenges or opportunities?
- Answer options: Very confident, Somewhat confident, Not very confident, Not at all confident

6. Do you regularly practice positive self-talk and affirmations?
- Answer options: Yes, No, Sometimes, Not Sure

7. How open are you to receiving feedback and constructive criticism?
- Answer options: Very open, Somewhat open, Not very open, Not at all open

8. How much do external factors, such as the opinions of others or fear of failure, influence your beliefs about yourself?
- Answer options: Not at all, A little, Somewhat, A lot

9. How willing are you to take risks and step outside of your comfort zone?
- Answer options: Very willing, Somewhat willing, Not very willing, Not at all willing

10. How often do you acknowledge and celebrate your own successes and accomplishments?
- Answer options: Always, Sometimes, Rarely, Never

Answers:
1.   Yes
2.   Rarely
3.   Use setbacks as opportunities to learn and grow
4.   Sometimes
5.   Very confident
6.   Yes
7.   Very open

8.   A little
9.   Very willing
10.   Sometimes

Self-belief exercise

Here's a self-belief exercise you can try:

1.   Take out a piece of paper and write down three things you've accomplished in the past that you're proud of. They can be big or small accomplishments, such as completing a project at work or learning a new skill.

2.   Next, write down three things you're currently working on or want to achieve in the future. Again, they can be big or small goals, such as finishing a book you've been meaning to read or getting a promotion at work.

3.   For each of the three things you've accomplished in the past, write down the qualities and skills that helped you achieve them. For example, if you completed a project at work, you might have used skills like organization, time management, and problem-solving.

4.   Now, think about how you can apply those same qualities and skills to the three goals you're currently working on. Write down specific actions you can take to use those skills to help you achieve your goals.

5.   Finally, write down a positive affirmation or mantra that reminds you of your abilities and strengths. For example, "I am capable and confident in my abilities to achieve my goals."

6.   Keep this paper somewhere you can see it often, such as on your desk or in your planner, to remind you of your past accomplishments and future goals, as well as your strengths and abilities.

Visualization exercise

Here's a simple visualization exercise that you can try:

1. Find a quiet and comfortable place to sit or lie down.

2. Close your eyes and take a few deep breaths to relax your body and mind.

3. Visualize yourself in a peaceful and serene environment, such as a beach or a forest. Use all your senses to immerse yourself in this environment, imagining the sound of the waves or the chirping of the birds, feeling the warmth of the sun on your skin or the coolness of the breeze.

4. Imagine yourself accomplishing your goals and living your dream life. See yourself happy, healthy, and fulfilled. Imagine the people around you, the places you visit, and the things you do.

5. Stay in this visualization for a few minutes, enjoying the positive feelings and emotions that arise.

6. When you're ready, slowly bring yourself back to the present moment and open your eyes.

7. You can repeat this exercise daily or as often as you like to help you stay focused on your goals and aspirations.

Chapter 5: Building Healthy Relationships and Networks

Building healthy relationships and networks is crucial for success in both personal and professional life. Positive relationships can provide emotional support, offer different perspectives and ideas, and provide opportunities for personal and professional growth. In contrast, toxic relationships can drain one's energy, damage self-esteem, and hinder progress towards goals.
Networking is also an essential aspect of building relationships and creating opportunities for success. Networking allows individuals to meet new people, develop connections with others in their field or industry, and potentially open doors to new career opportunities. It is essential to approach networking with a genuine interest in getting to know others and building relationships rather than just seeking personal gain.

Identifying toxic relationships

Identifying toxic relationships can be difficult, but some common signs to watch out for include:

1. **Consistent negativity:** If a person is constantly negative and critical of you or others, it may be a sign of toxicity.

2. **Controlling behavior:** If a person tries to control your actions, choices, or relationships, it may be a sign of toxicity.

3. **Lack of respect:** If a person consistently disrespects your boundaries or values, it may be a sign of toxicity.

4. **One-sidedness:** If a person only seems interested in their own

needs and doesn't show concern for your well-being, it may be a sign of toxicity.

5. **Manipulation:** If a person tries to manipulate you or guilt-trip you into doing things, it may be a sign of toxicity.

6. **Jealousy and competition:** If a person is constantly jealous of your successes or tries to compete with you, it may be a sign of toxicity.

It's important to remember that toxic behavior can come from anyone, including friends, family members, and romantic partners. If you notice these signs in a relationship, it may be necessary to set boundaries or even end the relationship for your own well-being.

Cultivating positive relationships

To cultivate positive relationships, consider the following tips:

1. **Practice active listening:** Be present in the conversation and give the other person your full attention. Listen to understand, not just to respond.

2. **Communicate effectively:** Be clear in your communication, express yourself in a respectful and positive way, and be open to feedback.

3. **Show appreciation and gratitude:** Express your appreciation and gratitude for the people in your life. Let them know how much you value them and the positive impact they have on your life.

4. **Build trust:** Be honest, reliable, and keep your commitments. Show that you are dependable and trustworthy.

5. **Be supportive:** Be there for the people in your life when they need you. Offer support, encouragement, and help when they need it.

6. **Respect boundaries:** Respect the boundaries of others and communicate your own boundaries clearly. This helps to build trust and respect in the relationship.

7. **Foster mutual growth:** Encourage personal growth and development in your relationships. Support each other in achieving your goals and aspirations.

Networking for success

Networking can be a powerful tool for achieving success in both personal and professional endeavors. Here are some tips for effective networking:

1. **Be genuine and authentic:** When networking, it's important to be genuine and authentic in your interactions with others. People can sense when someone is being insincere or fake, and this can harm your chances of building meaningful relationships.

2. **Build relationships, not just contacts:** Focus on building genuine relationships with people rather than just collecting business cards. Take the time to get to know people and their interests, and look for ways to help them achieve their goals.

3. **Attend events and conferences:** Attend events and conferences related to your field to meet new people and learn about the latest trends and developments in your industry.

4. **Use social media:** Social media platforms like Linked In can be valuable tools for networking. Use them to connect with people in your industry and join relevant groups.

5. **Follow up:** After meeting someone new, make sure to follow

up with them to keep the conversation going. Send an email or invite them to grab coffee to continue building the relationship.

Remember, networking is about building relationships, so focus on building genuine connections with people who can help you achieve your goals.

Relationship-building quiz

1. What is the first step to building a healthy relationship?
    A) Trust B) Communication
    C) Respect D) Honesty

2. Which of the following is NOT a sign of a toxic relationship?
    A) Feeling drained or exhausted after spending time with the person
    B) Being able to communicate openly and honestly with the person
    C) Feeling like you're walking on eggshells around the person
    D) Feeling like the person is always trying to control or manipulate you

3. How can you improve communication in a relationship?
    A) Avoid discussing sensitive topics B) Interrupt the person when they're speaking
    C) Practice active listening D) Criticize and blame the person for their behavior

4. What is the importance of empathy in relationships?
    A) It allows you to understand and connect with the other person's feelings
    B) It helps you control the other person's behavior
    C) It is not important in relationships
    D) It can lead to misunderstandings and conflicts

5. Which of the following is NOT a way to build trust in a relationship?
    A) Keeping promises and following through on commitments
    B) Being consistent in your words and actions

C) Being honest and transparent
D) Sharing personal information with strangers

6.   Which of the following is a sign of a healthy relationship?
  A) Feeling like you have to hide your true self from the other person
  B) Feeling like you're constantly trying to change the other person
  C) Feeling respected and appreciated by the other person
  D) Feeling like you always have to compromise your own values and beliefs

7.   How can you improve conflict resolution in a relationship?
  A) Avoid discussing sensitive topics
  B) Use physical force to get your point across
  C) Practice active listening and compromise
  D) Criticize and blame the other person for their behavior

8.   Which of the following is a sign of a toxic relationship?
  A) Feeling like you can't trust the other person
  B) Feeling respected and appreciated by the other person
  C) Feeling like you can communicate openly and honestly with the other person
  D) Feeling like you have equal power and control in the relationship

9.   Which of the following is NOT a way to maintain a healthy relationship?
  A) Spending quality time together
  B) Engaging in activities and hobbies separately
  C) Practicing forgiveness and letting go of grudges
  D) Criticizing and belittling the other person

10.   How can you build intimacy in a relationship?
  A) Avoiding physical touch and emotional vulnerability
  B) Communicating openly and honestly with the other person
  C) Keeping secrets and withholding information
  D) Criticizing and blaming the other person for their behavior

11.   Which of the following is NOT a way to show appreciation in

a relationship?
A) Saying "thank you" and expressing gratitude
B) Taking the other person for granted
C) Doing small acts of kindness for the other person
D) Giving compliments and showing affection

12. Which of the following is a sign of a healthy relationship?
A) Feeling like you always have to walk on eggshells around the other person
B) Feeling like you can communicate openly and honestly with the other person
C) Feeling like you have to change your personality to fit the other person's expectations
D) Feeling like you're constantly competing with the other person

13. Which of the following is a way to maintain a healthy relationship?
A) Keeping secrets and withholding information
B) Avoiding physical touch and emotional vulnerability
C) Practicing forgiveness and letting go of grudges
D) Criticizing and belittling the other person

Networking exercise:

Here is a networking exercise that you can try:

1. **Identify your networking goal:** Determine what you hope to achieve through networking. Are you looking for job opportunities, seeking mentorship, or trying to expand your professional network?

2. **Research your target audience:** Identify the individuals or groups that can help you achieve your networking goal. This can include industry professionals, alumni from your alma ater, or social media groups related to your field.

3. **Develop your elevator pitch:** Create a brief, compelling introduction that summarizes your skills, experience, and goals.

This should be no longer than 30 seconds and should leave a lasting impression on those you speak to.

4. **Attend networking events:** Look for local or online events that align with your networking goal. This can include industry conferences, meetups, or virtual networking events.

5. **Start a conversation:** Approach individuals or groups and introduce yourself using your elevator pitch. Ask open-ended questions to get to know them and show a genuine interest in their work or experiences.

6. **Follow up:** After the event, follow up with those you met and continue to build relationships. Connect on LinkedIn or send a personalized email to express your appreciation for their time and express your interest in keeping in touch.

Remember that networking is a two-way street, and it's essential to provide value to those you connect with. Be genuine, authentic, and proactive in your approach to networking, and you'll find that it can be a valuable tool for achieving your professional goals.

Chapter 6: Creating Work-Life Balance and Managing Stress

In today's fast-paced world, achieving a balance between work and personal life can be a daunting task. It's important to maintain a healthy balance between your professional and personal life to live a fulfilling and happy life. This chapter will focus on ways to create work-life balance and manage stress effectively.

Some of the topics covered in this chapter include:
- Strategies for managing stress
- Prioritizing self-care
- Achieving work-life balance

implementing the strategies and techniques outlined in this chapter, you can reduce stress and achieve a better balance between work and personal life, leading to increased productivity, better health, and overall happiness.

Strategies for managing stress

we will discuss some effective strategies for managing stress, which is essential for achieving work-life balance and maintaining good physical and mental health
.

1. **Practice mindfulness:** Mindfulness is the practice of being fully present in the moment and aware of your thoughts, feelings, and surroundings. Mindfulness can help you reduce stress and increase your ability to focus and concentrate. You can practice mindfulness by taking a few minutes each day to meditate or simply focus on your breathing.

2. **Exercise regularly:** Exercise is a great way to reduce stress

and improve your physical and mental health. Regular exercise can help you release tension, boost your mood, and improve your sleep quality. Try to aim for at least 30 minutes of moderate exercise each day.

3. **Get enough sleep:** Lack of sleep can contribute to stress, anxiety, and other health problems. Aim to get at least 7-8 hours of sleep each night to help your body and mind recharge.

4. **Take breaks:** Taking breaks throughout the day can help you recharge and reduce stress. Take a walk, read a book, or listen to music during your break to help you relax and recharge.

5. **Set boundaries:** Setting boundaries is important to maintain work-life balance. Learn to say no to requests that are not aligned with your values or priorities, and make time for the things that matter most to you.

6. **Practice self-care:** Practicing self-care is important for managing stress and improving your overall well-being. Make time for activities that you enjoy, such as reading, taking a bath, or practicing a hobby.

7. **Seek support:** Talking to a trusted friend, family member, or therapist can help you manage stress and improve your mental health. Don't hesitate to seek help if you need it.

Remember, managing stress is not a one-time event. It requires ongoing effort and practice. By incorporating these strategies into your daily routine, you can develop the resilience and coping skills needed to manage stress and achieve work-life balance.

Prioritizing self-care

Prioritizing self-care is essential for achieving and maintaining work-life balance and managing stress. Here are some strategies for prioritizing self-care:

1. **Make time for yourself:** Set aside time each day for

yourself, even if it's just 15 minutes. Use this time to do something that you enjoy or find relaxing, such as reading a book, taking a bath, or practicing yoga.

2. **Exercise regularly:** Exercise is a great way to reduce stress and improve your overall health. Make it a priority to exercise regularly, whether it's going to the gym, taking a walk, or participating in a sport.

3. **Get enough sleep:** Lack of sleep can contribute to stress and make it difficult to focus and be productive. Aim for 7-8 hours of sleep each night to feel rested and refreshed.

4. **Eat a healthy diet:** A healthy diet can help you feel better both physically and mentally. Aim to eat a balanced diet with plenty of fruits, vegetables, whole grains, and lean proteins.

5. **Connect with others:** Spending time with friends and family can help you feel more connected and supported, which can reduce stress and improve your mood.

6. **Set boundaries:** It's important to set boundaries with work and other commitments to avoid burnout. Learn to say "no" when necessary and prioritize your own needs and well-being.

Achieving work-life balance

Achieving work-life balance is crucial for maintaining overall well-being and success in both personal and professional life. Here are some strategies for achieving work-life balance:

1. **Set boundaries:** It is important to set clear boundaries between work and personal life. This can include setting specific work hours, taking breaks during the day, and avoiding work-related communication outside of work hours.

2. **Prioritize:** Prioritize your time and energy based on what is most important to you. This may mean saying no to certain commitments or delegating tasks.

3. **Make time for hobbies and leisure activities:** Engaging in hobbies or leisure activities outside of work can help to reduce stress and promote relaxation.

4. **Practice self-care:** Taking care of your physical and mental health is essential for achieving work-life balance. This can include getting enough sleep, exercising regularly, and practicing relaxation techniques such as meditation or yoga.

5. **Seek support:** It is important to have a support system, whether it be through family, friends, or colleagues. Don't be afraid to ask for help or support when needed.

By implementing these strategies, individuals can achieve a better balance between their personal and professional lives, leading to greater happiness and success.

Stress-management quiz:

here is a stress-management quiz:
1. How often do you feel overwhelmed or anxious?
   a) Rarely b) Sometimes c) Often d) Almost always

2. What is your typical response to stress?
   a) Avoidance b) Procrastination
   c) Seeking social support d) Exercise or other physical activity

3. How much sleep do you get each night?
   a) Less than 6 hours b) 6-8 hours
   c) More than 8 hours d) Varies each night

4. How often do you take breaks throughout the day?
   a) Never b) Rarely c) Sometimes d) Frequently

5. Do you practice any relaxation techniques, such as meditation or deep breathing?
   a) Yes, regularly b) Sometimes c) Rarely d) Never

6. How often do you engage in activities you enjoy?
   a) Daily b) Weekly c) Monthly d) Rarely

7. Do you feel like you have control over your daily schedule and tasks?
   a) Yes, always b) Sometimes c) Rarely d) Never

8. How often do you experience physical symptoms of stress, such as headaches or stomach aches?
   a) Rarely b) Sometimes c) Often d) Almost always

9. How often do you talk to someone about your stress or seek professional help?
   a) Regularly b) Sometimes c) Rarely d) Never

10. Do you have any regular self-care practices, such as taking a relaxing bath or reading a book?
    a) Yes, regularly b) Sometimes c) Rarely d) Never

Scoring:
1. a=1, b=2, c=3, d=4
2. a=1, b=2, c=3, d=4
3. a=4, b=2, c=1, d=3
4. a=1, b=2, c=3, d=4
5. a=4, b=3, c=2, d=1
6. a=4, b=3, c=2, d=1
7. a=4, b=3, c=2, d=1
8. a=1, b=2, c=3, d=4
9. a=4, b=3, c=2, d=1
10. a=4, b=3, c=2, d=1

Results: 10-20: Your stress-management techniques may need improvement. Consider seeking help or implementing new strategies. 21-30: You are on the right track, but there is room for improvement. Consider adding new stress-management techniques to your routine. 31-40: You are doing a great job managing your stress! Keep up the good work and continue to implement self-care practices.

Stress-management exercise

Here's a stress-management exercise that you can try:
1. Find a quiet and comfortable place where you won't be disturbed.

2. Sit or lie down in a comfortable position and take a few deep breaths.

3. Close your eyes and visualize a peaceful scene. This could be a beach, a forest, or any other place that brings you calm and relaxation.

4. Focus on your breathing and try to deepen it. Breathe in through your nose and out through your mouth.

5. As you continue to breathe deeply, scan your body for any areas of tension or discomfort. If you notice any, try to release the tension as you exhale.

6. Now, imagine yourself surrounded by a warm and soothing light. This light represents peace and relaxation.

7. As you bask in this light, repeat a positive affirmation to yourself, such as "I am calm and peaceful" or "I release all stress and tension."

8. Stay in this relaxed state for as long as you like, continuing to focus on your breath and the positive affirmations.

9. When you are ready, slowly open your eyes and take a few deep breaths before returning to your daily activities.

Remember, this is just one exercise that may help you manage stress. It's important to find what works best for you and to make stress management a regular part of your self-care routine.

Chapter 7: Reflection and Growth

After taking action towards our goals and implementing strategies to overcome obstacles, it is important to take time to reflect on our progress and assess what worked and what didn't work. This chapter focuses on the importance of reflection and growth in the journey towards unlocking our potential for success.

Some key topics covered in this chapter include:
- Taking time for reflection
- Making necessary adjustments to your plan of action
- Measuring progress and celebrating successes

Taking time for reflection

Taking time for reflection is crucial for personal growth and development. It allows us to look back on our experiences, successes, and failures, and gain insights that can inform our future decisions and actions. Reflection can help us identify patterns in our behavior or thought processes that may be hindering our progress or causing us unnecessary stress. It can also help us celebrate our achievements and appreciate the people and experiences that have supported us along the way.

To take time for reflection, set aside a specific time and space where you can be alone with your thoughts. This might involve taking a walk in nature, journaling, meditating, or simply sitting quietly and contemplating your experiences. Ask yourself open-ended questions, such as "What did I learn from this experience?" or "What could I have done differently?" Allow yourself to be honest and non-judgmental as you reflect, and try to approach your experiences with a growth mindset.

Making necessary adjustments to your plan of action

Making necessary adjustments to your plan of action is crucial for success. Reflection can help you identify areas where you are making progress and areas where you may need to adjust your strategy. Once you have identified areas where you need to make changes, you can revise your plan of action and continue moving forward. Remember, it's important to be flexible and willing to adapt as you work towards your goals. Don't be afraid to seek support or guidance from others as you navigate challenges and make changes to your plan. Keep a positive attitude and stay focused on your goals, and you will be on your way to success.

Measuring progress and celebrating successes

Measuring progress and celebrating successes is an important part of achieving your goals and unlocking your potential for success. Here are some tips for measuring progress and celebrating successes:

1. **Set milestones:** Break down your goals into smaller milestones that you can track and celebrate as you achieve them. This will help you stay motivated and feel a sense of accomplishment along the way.

2. **Use metrics:** Identify key metrics that you can use to measure your progress, such as sales figures, website traffic, or customer feedback. Keep track of these metrics over time and celebrate when you see improvements.

3. **Celebrate small wins:** Even small victories should be celebrated! Take time to acknowledge and celebrate the small wins along the way. This will help you stay motivated and build momentum towards your larger goals.

4. **Reflect on your achievements:** Take time to reflect on your achievements and how far you've come. This can help boost your confidence and give you the motivation you need to keep pushing forward.

Remember, measuring progress and celebrating successes is not just about achieving your goals, it's also about enjoying the journey and recognizing your hard work and dedication.

Measuring progress quiz

1. Why is it important to measure progress towards your goals?
   A. To determine if you are on track to achieving your goals.
   B. To hold yourself accountable.
   C. To identify areas where you may need to make adjustments.
   D. All of the above.
   Answer: D. All of the above.

2. How often should you measure progress towards your goals?
   A. Every month. B. Every week.
   C. Every day. D. It depends on the goal and timeline.
   Answer: D. It depends on the goal and timeline.

3. What are some ways to measure progress towards your goals?
   A. Tracking metrics and data. B. Conducting regular self-assessments.
    C. Seeking feedback from others. D. All of the above.
   Answer: D. All of the above.

4. What is a SMART goal?
   A. A goal that is specific, measurable, achievable, relevant, and time-bound.
   B. A goal that is simple, memorable, actionable, realistic, and timely.
   C. A goal that is strategic, meaningful, ambitious, realistic, and timely.
   D. A goal that is structured, measurable, actionable, relevant, and timely.
   Answer: A. A goal that is specific, measurable, achievable, relevant, and time-bound.

5. How can celebrating small wins along the way help with measuring progress?
   A. It helps to motivate you to keep going.
   B. It provides a sense of accomplishment and boosts confidence.

C. It allows you to see the progress you've made towards your larger goal.
D. All of the above.
Answer: D. All of the above.

Self-reflection exercise

Here's a self-reflection exercise you can try:
1. Find a quiet and comfortable space where you can reflect without interruptions.
2. Take a few deep breaths and allow yourself to relax.
3. Think about your recent experiences, both positive and negative.
4. Ask yourself the following questions:
5. What did I learn from this experience?
6. How did it make me feel?
7. What could I have done differently?
8. What did I do well?
9. What do I want to continue doing or improve upon in the future?

1. Write down your answers in a journal or notebook.
2. Take a few more deep breaths and express gratitude for the opportunity to reflect and learn.
3. Repeat this exercise regularly to continue learning and growing.

Remember to be kind and compassionate with yourself as you reflect on your experiences. The goal of this exercise is not to criticize yourself, but to learn and grow from your experiences.

Rise Up and Shine: Unlocking Your Potential for Success is a guide book for anyone who wants to achieve their goals and live their best life. By focusing on the power of self-belief, positive thinking, goal setting, overcoming fear and negative self-talk, building confidence and resilience, and creating healthy relationships and work-life balance, this book provides practical tips and techniques for personal and professional growth.

Remember that success is not a destination, but a journey. It requires hard work, determination, and a willingness to learn and grow. With the tools and strategies outlined in this book, you can unlock your full potential and achieve the success you deserve.

Keep in mind that everyone's path to success is different, and there may be obstacles and setbacks along the way. But with a positive attitude, a clear vision of your goals, and a commitment to taking action, you can overcome any challenge and rise to new heights.

So, don't be afraid to take risks, try new things, and step out of your comfort zone. Embrace your unique talents and strengths, and let them shine. With dedication and perseverance, you can achieve anything you set your mind to. Rise up and shine!